Melleron's Monsters

Douglas Hill

Illustrated by Steve Hutton

OXFORD
UNIVERSITY PRESS

For my grandson
DECLAN
and also of course for Rose

Land of the
Stonewall
Foo
the Peaceful
IRON OAK
CLEARING
Western
Grassland
Farm

MONSTERS
OUNTAINS
ILLS
orest
SILVERBERRY GROVE
Melleron's Cottage
Village
NDS

CHAPTER 1

Strange travellers

The two small creatures had travelled a long way, across a wild, grim, difficult land – one trotting on four sturdy legs, the other floating on delicate wings.

Because they knew they might be pursued, they had travelled mostly at night, through the shelter of gullies and ravines, woods and thick brush. All of that had made their journey longer and harder. And the hardest part of all had come when they reached the massive range of the Stonewall Mountains, with its craggy ridges and looming cliffs.

But they kept on, at last finding their way through a deep canyon between towering walls of stone. Beyond that lay the downward slopes on the far side of the mountains, where they could move faster. So, before long, they came to the top of a grassy ridge near the foot of the mountains, where they stopped to gaze at what lay ahead.

An enormous, splendid forest, spreading as far as they could see.

'There it is,' said the winged one, settling on to a rocky outcrop. 'Just where it's supposed to be.'

They had arrived at dawn, so the forest still looked like a solid dark mass. The few streaks of grey light in the eastern clouds were not enough to show the many paths and glades, the spaces among the trees and thickets. But as they gazed, they could hear the first sleepy chirps of birds among that vast spread of branches, tuning up their voices to greet the morning.

'It's *bigger* than I expected,' the winged one went on. 'I've never *seen* a forest that huge.'

The other one nodded.

'So it's *perfect,*' the winged one said. 'If anyone does come after us, they'll *never* find us here. And we'll be able to keep away from *people*, too.'

The other one made a sound like a throaty growl.

'Right,' the winged one said, smiling. *'They'd* better keep away from *us*.' The smile became a quiet laugh. 'Did you know they call it the *Peaceful* Forest? Just what we could do with, for now – a bit of peace.'

The other one growled again, but the sound was tinged with laughter.

Then they set off down the slope towards the forest, where the birdsong was rising in full chorus as if to welcome them as well as the dawn.

At about the same time, a long way westward from the forest, two other beings were talking, within a stone house half-hidden at the foot of a hill. One of them was a bone-thin man wearing a stained purple cloak, its hood shadowing his face. The other was huge and bulky and hairy, and not human at all.

'Are you saying I should *stop*?' the hairy one was saying, in a rumbling growl.

'Certainly not,' the hooded one said sharply. 'You can go on raiding farms and killing sheep and attacking people as much as you like. I'm

merely saying that you should widen your range – to the lands east of here.' His eyes glittered within the hood's shadow. 'Men from those eastern lands came to help drive me away, forcing me to live in this wilderness. They must suffer too.'

'If you wish,' the hairy one rumbled. 'It is all the same to me.'

'Of course, at that distance,' the hooded one went on, 'I'll no longer be able to cover your tracks and keep you hidden . . .'

'I have no need to hide,' the hairy one broke in.

'Don't be stupid,' the hooded one snapped. 'Are you so eager to face a large troop of people, angry and determined and well-armed?' As the other subsided into muttering, he waved a skinny hand. 'There is a vast forest in that area, the Peaceful Forest. You can hide in its depths, between attacks. The people in that region fear the forest, and rarely venture in.'

The hairy one grunted. 'If I could raise the *army* that I dream of, there would be no need of hiding.'

'That may happen yet,' the hooded one snarled. 'We have only just begun. While you are ravaging, I will be laying my plans and readying my powers.' His laugh was low and chilling. 'When we are done with them, all these farmland fools will most bitterly regret their treatment of me.'

'And of my kind,' the hairy one rumbled.

'Indeed.' The hooded one fumbled in a pocket of his cloak. 'Now – should you need to make contact with me . . .'

From the pocket he brought out a green stone, and spoke a harsh strange word. The stone rose magically into the air, then was suddenly hanging from a thin chain like a pendant, around the hairy one's neck.

'Simply hold the stone in your hand,' the hooded one said, 'and say my name.'

The hairy one nodded, peering down at his new pendant, baring huge fangs in a cruel grin. 'And you say it is called the Peaceful Forest, where I am going? I wonder how peaceful it will seem when people know that *I* am in it.'

CHAPTER 2

Forest paths

As soon as he awoke, Melleron went to his window, pleased to see a bright warm morning. Just what was wanted for the first day after the village school closed for the summer. He gazed happily out at the forest that grew all around the cottage, its leaves and branches moving in a breeze like many-fingered green hands, beckoning him.

'I'll be there as soon as I can,' he murmured, and dashed from his room.

As he burst into the kitchen, his grandmother – slightly stooped and thin with wispy white hair – turned with a smile. 'What's your hurry?'

'I can hardly wait to get into the forest,' Melleron said.

'The forest isn't going anywhere,' the old woman said teasingly. 'Breakfast first. And school being out doesn't mean chores stop.'

Melleron could think of many things he would rather do besides chores, on the first day of summer break. But the work had to be done, and there was only himself and Nan to do it. In fact Melleron was ready to do more than his share, for Nan was getting a bit shaky as she grew older.

So, after breakfast, they got on with clearing up, sweeping the floor, chopping some kindling and so on. Then they went out together to tackle a patch of tangleweed that had invaded the vegetable garden.

Melleron was a fairly ordinary-looking boy of eleven, with thick dark hair and large dark eyes, perhaps small for his age, and thin. But he was wiry rather than spindly, so that an hour of hacking with a hoe at the tough weed in the warm sun didn't trouble him. It was harder on Nan, though, who finally stopped, mopped her brow and declared that that was enough for one day.

So at last Melleron was free to dash away into the depths of the place that he loved best – the enormous expanse of greenery called the Peaceful Forest.

It had been given that name in the olden days, after the Monster War, when the enemy army of monstrous creatures had finally been driven back over the Stonewall Mountains. In those last battles, the humans also almost accidentally cleared all *other* dangerous creatures out of their lands, including the forest. All the howler-bears, blood-wolves, two-tailed vipers and the rest disappeared forever.

By Melleron's day the forest held nothing worse than little bushcats and pad-foxes, blue owls and swallow-hawks. And none of those was any danger to people.

Yet even so, people hardly ever went into the forest, because of the remembered terrors of the long-ago war – and because beyond the forest lay the mountains, and beyond the mountains lay the nightmare land of the monsters.

In fact, since the war, not one monster had ever been seen in the forest or in any other part of the human lands. All the same, most people still saw the forest as a spooky, scary place, and avoided it.

But not everyone. A few people knew that the Peaceful Forest was truly peaceful, holding no dangers. And Nan was one of the few. She and Melleron's grandfather had lived in the forest for many long years, for the grandfather had been a hunter, a woodcutter, a gatherer of nuts and berries and wild honey.

So Melleron – who had lived with his grandparents from babyhood – had been learning the ways of the forest almost all his life. And now that he was nearly twelve, Nan never worried at all about him going alone, to wander the green-shaded paths.

It was the best time of year, Melleron thought, for wandering in the forest. The trees wore their richest midsummer green, splashed with colour from bushes and wild flowers. And the air was filled with the endless voice of the forest – the song of birds, the hum of insects, the creak of branches, the whisper of the breeze.

So Melleron gazed and listened happily as he moved along the familiar paths, heading first for one of his favourite places – a clearing at the heart of the forest. There a giant ancient iron-oak tree, mostly dead, tilted steeply towards its final fall.

'Not fallen yet?' Melleron said aloud, patting the iron-oak's craggy bark. But he knew it wouldn't be much longer, for even the mild breeze that morning was making the old tree shudder and creak.

From the clearing Melleron's wandering brought him to a clump of paint-willows that was home to a tree-mouse family. As he drew near, he saw a mouse suddenly fall from one tree, then creep slowly away along the ground, dragging one leg.

Melleron smiled, for he had seen the trick before. There would be young mice in a nest – so the mother was *pretending* to be hurt, to lure a possible attacker away from them. And indeed, after he had followed her awhile, the mother mouse whisked up another tree, with no sign of injury, and vanished among the leaves.

By then Melleron was feeling hungry, so he followed other paths to a grove filled with silverberry bushes, which always had some ripe fruit on their branches, any time of year. Eagerly he reached for a cluster of the big juicy-sweet berries.

As he did so he heard a startling, unusual sound, very near. A sound like '*rrrr*'. A warning growl.

CHAPTER 3

Dangerous creatures

Melleron wasn't really alarmed by the growl, just curious. Probably a bushcat, he thought, letting me know it's around. He stood still, peering into the bushes.

'Don't worry, whatever you are,' he murmured. 'I won't hurt you.'

He thought that he heard something like a sniff, but saw nothing. Straightening, he noticed another visitor to the grove. Some kind of bird, fluttering around a bush, snatching at berries.

As far as Melleron could see, through the leaves, it was about the size of a bush-pigeon.

But bush-pigeons didn't eat silverberries. And this bird, when Melleron caught a clearer glimpse, had something strange about its beak and its legs. Even stranger, it seemed to be a bright astonishing *pink*, all over.

He had never seen or heard of a pink bird. So he crept around the bushes to get a closer look. But the fluttering pink thing somehow spotted him, and whirled away among the treetops.

'No, no – come back, pretty pink bird,' Melleron said, aloud.

At once he again heard the strange low growl, nearby, sounding even more like a warning.

In the next instant the pink bird-like thing swooped back into view – flashing down towards him like an arrow from a bow.

And it was *shrieking*. Actual words, in a high clear voice.

'Not pink! Not *pink*!' it shrieked. 'Don't you *dare* call me *pink*!'

And from its mouth – not a beak at all, Melleron saw, but a mouth with tiny sharp fangs – exploded a burst of blazing hot, bright blue fire.

In panic, Melleron tried to leap away. But netferns tangled his ankles, and he fell backwards with a cry as the stream of blue fire scorched the twigs above his head.

Yet despite his shock he was still staring at the pink creature. And astonishment overcame fright as he saw its four little legs with clawed feet, its crested head with the small fanged muzzle, its delicate wings, its snaky, spiky little tail, all covered not with feathers but with a smooth sort of *scaliness* . . .

'You're a *dragon*!' he cried.

The pink creature swung around and settled on a branch, glaring at him with bright eyes that were exactly the same shade of blue as the flame it had blasted out.

'Of *course* I'm a dragon!' it said in its high clear voice. 'And you're . . .'

But it paused as another creature stepped from the brush. This one looked like a little dog – sturdy and stocky, with a blunt muzzle and a stubby tail, short thick claws and sharp shiny teeth. But, strangely, it had no fur, and its bare skin looked as rough and weathered as old stone.

And it was moving forward, teeth bared, growling its low '*rrrr*'.

But the dragon flared its wings. 'No, Grit,' it said. 'It's just a *boy*.'

Melleron was still staring, fearful and amazed. 'Are you . . . have you come from beyond the mountains?' he stammered.

'Where else?' the dragon hissed, switching its spiky tail.

'What are you doing here?' Melleron asked breathlessly.

'That's none of your business,' the dragon snapped. 'Anyway, we won't *be* here much longer, thanks to you.'

'What do you mean?' Melleron asked, puzzled.

'I mean when you tell everyone about us, we'll have to *leave*,' the dragon said.

Melleron got slowly to his feet, still astounded but less fearful. The two small creatures were very strange, and not very friendly, but they no longer seemed to be threatening him. Even though they were from the land of the monsters . . .

And they were the most exciting thing that had ever happened to him.

'What if,' he said thoughtfully, 'I *didn't* tell anyone about you?'

The dragon fluttered down to a lower branch. 'Why wouldn't you?'

'Maybe I don't want crowds of people tramping through the forest, looking for you,' Melleron said. 'And maybe I don't think you're really dangerous . . .'

'Rrrrr!' said the little dog-creature, baring shiny teeth.

The dragon's blue eyes glinted. 'Grit wants you to know that we can be *very* dangerous.'

'I'm sure,' Melleron said quickly. 'I just meant that I don't think you'd start attacking people or anything. Even though you did try to burn me when I called you p . . . that word.'

'That word always makes me furious,' the dragon hissed. *'Rose* is my colour, and Rose is my *name*. That other word makes everyone think of sweet girly baby things, and I'm not. I'm Rose, and roses have thorns.'

'I'll remember,' Melleron promised.

'Don't bother,' Rose the dragon sniffed. 'You'll most likely never see us again.'

'But I've said I'm not going to tell anyone about you,' Melleron said wistfully. 'So why can't you stay?'

'Because,' Rose told him, 'whatever you say *now*, once you're back with other humans you'll be *bursting* to tell them about us. It's how people are.'

'I won't!' Melleron said. 'I promise!'

'And,' Rose went on, ignoring his promise, 'if the news got out that we're here, it would be very dangerous for us. It could even be the *end* of us.'

With that she swirled into the air, while Grit leaped back into the brush, and both vanished from sight.

CHAPTER 4

Misunderstandings

'Wait!' Melleron cried, shocked by the sudden disappearance. 'Rose, don't go! Stay and talk some more! Please! Come back . . . !'

But though he stayed there for some time, calling, and then searched through the forest around the grove, he failed to see any flashes of pink or to hear any growls. At last he gave up and trailed back to the cottage – tingling with the excitement of meeting the amazing little creatures, hoping that they wouldn't leave, wishing that he might see them again.

I didn't even tell them my name, he thought.

And there's so much I want to ask them – especially why they're here, why they left the land of the monsters . . . Though *they* aren't really monsters. They're too small, and not at all horrible. Not like the ones in the war.

In fact, he thought, Rose and Grit seem mostly anxious to *hide,* as if they're afraid. But what could be frightening them?

At home, Nan was pottering in the kitchen, cheerfully chatty, hardly noticing that Melleron seemed silent and thoughtful.

'Next time you go to the forest,' Nan said, 'could you pick a bag of silverberries? Then you could take them and some sweetbeans from the garden to sell in the village. We need flour and salt, and a wick for the lamp.'

Melleron sighed. He didn't want to do anything in the forest but try to find Rose and Grit again. And going to the village was not something he ever enjoyed. Still, like the chores, it had to be done, and it was easier for him than Nan.

So next morning after breakfast he rushed back into the forest, heading straight for the silverberry grove, eagerly hoping to spot a flash of pink among the leaves. But he saw and heard no sign of the two small creatures, anywhere in the area.

Glumly he began picking berries, filling the cloth bag he had brought. But then, instead of going straight home, he set off along the forest paths. The village can wait, he thought. I'm going to look for Rose and Grit.

Yet over the next hour or so he saw nothing but a few long-eared harelings. When he tried calling, he merely startled a flock of striped jays. Until at last, disappointed, he turned towards home – and stumbled as he turned, on a large jagged stone.

A very odd stone, he thought, peering at it. It looked like a chunk of flint, but it was lying in the middle of a mossy path, with no other stones or outcrops of rock anywhere near. And it had strange marks all over it. Almost like . . . *teeth* marks.

He bent to pick up the flint. As he straightened, he heard a crackle of twigs, a very loud growl that was almost a roar – and Grit burst out of the bushes, charging towards him, fangs glittering.

Shocked, Melleron dropped the flint and jumped back, hearing Rose's voice – 'No, Grit, wait!' – from the forest. At once Grit pounced on the stone, picking it up in his jaws, glaring, while Rose swooped into view, settling on a branch.

'He thought you were stealing his dinner,' she told Melleron.

'Dinner?' Melleron said blankly. 'A *stone*?'

'Why not?' Rose asked. 'You're made of meat and you *eat* meat – he's made of stone and he eats stone. He *loves* a nice piece of flint.'

'He's *made* of stone?' Melleron echoed, even more amazed.

'Rrr,' Grit said proudly.

'Certainly,' Rose said. '*Hard* stone, too. That's why he's very strong, for his size. And his teeth are *diamonds*.'

Melleron stared at Grit's bright teeth gripping the flint. And for a moment the little creature, looking back at him, seemed to wag his stubby tail.

'Now,' Rose demanded, 'why are you going around shouting out our names? Are you *trying* to let people know we're here?'

'No!' Melleron gasped. 'I *wouldn't* . . . Anyway, there's no one else around. I just wanted to see you again – to get to know you, to be *friends* . . .'

'*Friends*?' Rose repeated. 'With a *human*?'

'We could be,' Melleron insisted. 'You and Grit are friends, aren't you? Even though he's a stone dog and you're a p . . .'

'*Watch* it,' Rose snapped.

'A rose-coloured dragon,' Melleron said quickly.

Rose sniffed. 'Don't you have enough *human* friends?'

'I don't really have any friends at all,' Melleron muttered.

Rose peered at him, her fierce blue gaze softening a little. 'If that's true,' she began, 'I'm sorry for you . . .'

But then she stopped. From the forest, quite nearby, they heard a voice. A human voice, calling. '*Mell*-eronnnnn . . .!'

Grit growled, and Rose swooped furiously into the air. 'No one around, did you say?' she cried. 'Liar! You've been *leading* people here all along!'

'No!' Melleron said desperately. 'It's only my Nan . . .!'

But he was talking to empty air, because they had vanished into the greenery.

CHAPTER 5

Troubling news

That's done it, Melleron thought dolefully. They'll never trust me, after that. And he turned away, drooping, as Nan appeared on the path.

'I thought you'd got lost,' she said cheerily. 'Did you forget you were going to go to the village?'

'No,' Melleron mumbled. 'I was just coming.'

Gloomily he went with Nan back to the cottage, where she packed up vegetables from the garden into the bag with the silverberries. Still gloomily he carried it out to their rickety little barn, where he put a bridle on their bony old horse, clambered up bareback and rode away.

The dirt road beyond their cottage, winding among fields and meadows, was every bit as familiar to him as the paths in the forest. He rode that way to the village every day, during the school year. But he never enjoyed the journey, just as he never much enjoyed arriving.

Because, as he had told Rose, he didn't have any *friends* in school or in the village. Or anywhere else.

Melleron's grandfather had died some years before, leaving the boy and his Nan on their own. And they were all the more alone because Nan's cottage stood by itself within the fringes of the forest, some miles away from the village.

The villagers had always thought that Nan was odd, living apart from everyone, raising her grandson in the scary forest all by herself. But the cottage was Nan's home, and she had no intention of leaving. Even though, as time went on, she and Melleron began to be quite *poor*.

Nan tried to earn a living from the forest as her husband had done, hunting and gathering and wood-cutting. But she wasn't as strong or skilled as her husband had been, and she barely scraped by. And as she grew older, and more shaky, she and Melleron earned less and less.

They would never starve, while they had the forest and their garden. But they had little to spare for other things. The cottage was rundown, their only transport was the bony horse and a battered cart, and everything they owned was old and much-mended. Melleron's clothes, for instance, were mostly made-over things of his grandfather's – ill-fitting, patched and tattered.

So the local people sneered at them – 'those ragged scarecrows from the forest' – or just ignored them. And it was the same for Melleron at school, where some of the children mocked him, and the rest left him alone.

Melleron always told himself that it didn't matter. Being *alone,* he learned, wasn't always the same thing as being *lonely*. Besides, he had Nan, and he had the forest. And he felt that he wouldn't give up the forest for all the friends in the world.

And now the forest seemed even more precious to him. Because of the two marvellous creatures he had met there.

It was a slow hour's ride to the village, and as the horse ambled along Melleron day-dreamed about becoming friends with Rose and Grit. They might stay, he thought, if they learn that I haven't told anyone, that I can keep a secret.

As long as they don't leave, he thought gloomily, *before* they learn it.

In the village he had no trouble selling the berries and vegetables to the owner of the general store, using the money to buy the things they needed. One or two villagers nodded to him distantly, the storekeeper was neither friendly nor unfriendly, and everyone else ignored him.

But then he overheard some men talking – and the words of one big bearded man stopped Melleron short.

'They reckon somethin' dangerous has come out of the mountains, from the land of the monsters,' the man said.

Nervously, Melleron pretended to study a display of socks, listening. But to his surprise, the group wasn't talking about Rose or Grit or anything in the forest.

'Yeah, somethin' huge and hairy, I heard,' another man said. 'Attackin' folks, killin' livestock – all over the grasslands west of here.'

'Sounds like a howler-bear,' a third man muttered. 'Except there's none left.'

'And there's somethin' weird about this thing,' the bearded man said. 'Folks have *seen* it, but they can't *track* it. Like it leaves no trail or sign at all.'

'Remember,' the second man said, 'when some of our lads went over to the west to help chase off that sorcerer, Saelez? They say he's still skulkin' in the hills near there. Maybe he's got somethin' to do with this monster.'

The third man scowled. 'Let's just hope the thing stays away from here. We don't want any monsters settin' up home in the *forest*.'

CHAPTER 6

A different threat

As the men drifted away, Melleron left the store, troubled and puzzled. Could there really be another monster around? And did it have anything to do with Rose and Grit?

The questions were whirling in his mind as he took his bag of shopping back to his waiting horse. Where he was startled to find someone standing in his way.

Three bigger, older boys, lounging beside the horse, grinning. Three youths who, when they had been in school, had found cruel amusement in tormenting him.

'Look who's here!' one of them said loudly. His name was Waddel, Melleron knew – a squat boy with close-set eyes.

'It's Ragsy!' jeered another of them – a stringy, toothy boy named Pulce. 'Hey, Ragsy – you buyin' yourself a new suit?'

'Prob'ly buyin' more rags,' sneered the third one – Jackar, the leader, taller and broader than either of his friends.

Melleron tried to move around them, but Jackar stepped in front of him again. 'Let's see what you got in the bag, Ragsy,' he snarled.

'Yeah, we'll help you carry it,' Pulce said, snickering. 'It looks too heavy for a little skinny kid.'

He tried to grab the bag, but Melleron jerked it away. 'Leave me alone!' he said, glaring. 'Get away from my horse!'

'Whatever you say,' Jackar drawled – and slapped the horse powerfully on the rump. With a startled squeal, it leaped away, bolting along the street, vanishing around a building.

The three youths laughed cruelly. 'You can walk,' Jackar told Melleron. 'You'll prob'ly go faster than that bag of bones you call a horse.'

Melleron clenched his teeth, saying nothing. Around them, a few villagers were looking on, some with indifference, a few with half-smiles. But then from their midst strode a tall grey-haired man with anger in his eyes.

'You three feeling proud of yourselves,' he snapped, 'picking on someone so much smaller?'

Jackar and the other two scowled and backed away. The grey-haired man, whose name was Aldin, was the head of the village council and a district judge.

'You,' the judge said to Jackar. 'Fetch the boy's horse back, right away!'

'There's no need,' Melleron said, and whistled piercingly. At once, with a willing whicker, the horse came trotting back along the street towards him.

As Melleron reached for its bridle, the trio of bullies slunk away. And Judge Aldin turned to Melleron.

'Are you all right, son?' he asked.

'Yes, sir,' Melleron said, climbing on to the horse's back.

The judge nodded. 'Take

care, then. Say hello to your grandmother for me.'

'I will,' Melleron said. 'Thank you.'

Riding through the village, he saw no further sign of his three enemies. And out on the open road, while the horse went quietly along, Melleron drifted into another day-dream – about somehow luring Jackar and the others into the forest to meet Rose and Grit, and making Jackar say the word 'pink' . . .

But the dream ended with a jolt, when the horse snorted and came to a sudden halt that almost pitched Melleron from its back.

Jackar and his friends had stepped from behind a bush into the road ahead of him, glowering.

'You went and got us into trouble, Ragsy,' Jackar growled. 'So now we're goin' to give you trouble. And this time nobody's around to stop us.'

Pale and silent, Melleron watched the trio advance. Then, without warning, he whistled piercingly again, kicking his heels into the horse's bony flanks.

The sudden shock made the horse squeal and leap forward. As the startled youths tried to get out of its way, Melleron swung the bag of shopping like a club. Dodging back from it, Jackar crashed into Waddel and sent him flying, just as the horse's shoulder slammed into Pulce.

Galloping wildly on, Melleron glanced back. One of his enemies was sprawled and groaning in the road – but Jackar was shaking a furious fist.

'We'll get you!' the big youth yelled. 'An' when we do, we'll *smash* you!'

CHAPTER 7

Making friends

Chilled by the threat, Melleron urged the horse on. When he reached home, pale and tense on a sweaty horse, Nan hurried out to find out what was wrong. And when Melleron told her about the youths, her eyes blazed with fury.

'Cowards and thugs!' she cried. 'They ought to get a whipping! I've a mind to go and see to them myself!'

'No, Nan,' Melleron begged. 'Don't do anything.'

She clenched wrinkled fists. 'And the others in the village are no better, standing and watching . . .'

'Except the judge,' Melleron said.

Nan sighed and nodded. 'He's a good man, Judge Aldin . . . Well, you just stay away from the village awhile, and those louts will probably forget all about you.'

Melleron doubted it, but he was happy to avoid the village for as long as possible. So he tried to put the bullies out of his mind, which wasn't difficult, with Rose and Grit to think about instead.

The next day was warm but cloudy, with a threat of rain in the air. But Melleron refused to let his mood be dampened. After breakfast and chores, he slipped eagerly away, back to the forest pathways – roaming, searching, calling as before. Along the way he filled his pockets with silverberries, and picked up a large smooth stone with bright gleaming flecks.

But as an hour passed, and then another and another, there was no sign of them at all. Not in the silverberry grove, not in the grassy clearing where the old iron-oak tree leaned, not in any shaded dells or sunny glades, not on the path where he had met them before. Not anywhere.

At last, with the day growing even more humid, Melleron stopped by a clear little brook. By then he was drooping miserably, since his failure to find them meant either they didn't want anything to do with him, or they had left the forest. And he didn't know which would make him more unhappy.

Sadly he spread out the silverberries and the bright stone on a patch of moss. 'A picnic with no one to eat it,' he muttered, aloud.

Then he nearly fell into the brook, when a voice spoke behind him.

'To eat what?' the voice asked.

And as he spun around, Rose and Grit appeared from a thicket.

'Have you been watching me all this time?' Melleron demanded.

'Not *all* the time,' Rose said. 'We were ranging around, to see if there were *other* people in the forest with you, looking for us.'

'There aren't!' Melleron said firmly. 'It was only my Nan, last time, looking for *me*. I said I wouldn't tell anyone about you, and I haven't!'

'We know that now,' Rose said, her voice softening. 'We've been expecting to see hunters, or traps by the berry bushes . . . But there's been *nothing.*' She smiled. 'So you're a boy who keeps his promises. What's your *name,* anyway?'

'Melleron,' he said. 'And I really do want to be your friend.'

'We've never had a human friend,' Rose said. 'But if we're going to stay here awhile, we might *need* one. Mightn't we, Grit?'

'Rrrr,' Grit said, wagging his tail. 'Rrr, rrr,' he added.

'He wants to know about the *picnic* you mentioned,' Rose said.

'Is he really talking when he growls?' Melleron wondered.

'Oh, yes,' Rose said. 'He can't manage to *speak* this language, but he can follow most of what we're saying. He may be stone, but he's not *stupid*.'

'That's amazing,' Melleron breathed.

'Not really,' Rose said lightly. 'There are *lots* of monsters stranger than Grit and me, in the land beyond the mountains.'

'But you're not monsters . . .' Melleron said.

'*Rrrr!*' Grit said loudly.

Rose smiled. 'Grit says *he* is. And I suppose I am too. People would say dragons are monsters *whatever* size they are. Or colour.'

'But monsters are supposed to be ugly and horrible, and you're not,' Melleron said.

'Thank you,' Rose said. 'But ugly doesn't always mean *horrible*. There are *nice* monsters as well as the other sort.' She flapped her wings briskly, as if sweeping that topic aside. 'Now, what about this *picnic*?'

So they settled by the patch of moss, where Melleron and Rose devoured the berries while Grit happily crunched the stone like a dog with a bone. Melleron was also bubbling with questions, but his very first one brought a disturbing answer.

He asked why they had come to the forest. And Rose told him, with a shadow of fear in her blue eyes.

'We're here,' she said, 'to stay out of the way of an enemy – who is one of the most *truly* ugly and horrible monsters ever.'

CHAPTER 8

New fears

'His name is Horrimal,' Rose went on. 'He's almost twice as tall as a man, huge and powerful, covered with thick dark hair – and he has horns, evil yellow eyes, long claws, and a mouthful of fangs.'

Melleron gulped. 'Why is he your enemy?' he asked.

'Because we got him into deep *trouble,*' Rose said. 'Horrimal has been going around for *ages* spouting about how all monsters should get together and attack the humans again, to take *revenge* for their defeat in the Monster War . . .'

'That's terrible!' Melleron cried, pale and wide-eyed.

Rose waved a wing. 'Most other monsters just *ignore* him, except for a few of his friends – big and fierce and not too bright, like him. But lately, it seems, Horrimal has been secretly trying to get his friends to join him in a sort of *raiding* party. To do as much harm as possible, here on the human lands.'

Melleron went even paler as a terrible thought struck him.

'As it turned out,' Rose went on before he could speak, 'no one *wanted* to join him. But he didn't give up. Then one night Grit and I *overheard* him, going on about it to his gang – and we thought we ought to tell the Chief of the monsters, who was so angry that he had Horrimal *chained* in a cave, to stop him doing anything stupid.'

'But he's not there now . . .' Melleron whispered.

'How did you guess?' Rose said, surprised. 'No, he escaped. Some said he had *help* from somewhere. Anyway, the others thought he might come after Grit and me, because we discovered his plan. So the Chief said we should *leave* and find a place to lie low awhile, till everything calmed down.'

'Rrrrr,' Grit said angrily.

'Grit wanted to stay and *fight*,' Rose said.

'Fight a huge terrible monster?' Melleron gasped.

'Grit will fight *anything*, if he's angry enough,' Rose said, her eyes flashing. 'So will I, if it comes to that. But anyway, here we are in your Peaceful Forest, while Horrimal is probably looking all over the mountains for us.'

Melleron shivered. 'Maybe he isn't . . .' And he told them what he had heard in the village, about the huge hairy creature prowling the grasslands to the west.

'That sounds like Horrimal,' Rose said calmly. 'He'd *enjoy* attacking farms and all that. And if there's a wicked *sorcerer* over there, as you say, maybe they're linked up. Maybe the sorcerer was the one who helped Horrimal escape.'

'You don't seem very bothered,' Melleron said.

'Rrr, rrr,' Grit remarked.

'That's right,' Rose said. 'We're not. After all, Horrimal isn't *here,* in the forest – and he won't have any idea that *we're* here. Anyway, if he goes on ravaging, the people will probably hunt him down and solve *everyone's* problems.'

'Rrrrr,' Grit growled.

Rose laughed. 'No, Grit, I *don't* think they would let us join the hunt.'

That made them all laugh, and the laughter swept away their worries. Finishing their picnic, they wandered the paths together, talking peacefully. At one point Melleron joked that Rose would have to be careful, in the autumn, about breathing fire when the leaves were dry. But her reply surprised him.

'I can't do it whenever I *want*,' she said, seeming embarrassed, though it was hard to tell since she was already pink. 'It only happens when I get really *furious*.'

'Rrr!' Grit said brightly.

Rose laughed. 'Grit says I have a *fiery* temper . . .'

So they chatted on, until it was time for Melleron to be getting home. 'Can I come and see you tomorrow?' he asked.

'Come *any* time,' Rose said cheerily. 'Just be sure you always come *alone*.'

On his way home Melleron's mind was awhirl with all the things he had learned about his amazing new friends. It looked like being a wonderful summer, he thought.

Unless something went wrong – if Rose and

Grit were discovered, or if the monster Horrimal found out where they were . . . So an edge of worry cast its shadow.

And back at the cottage there was another worry, another shadow.

'Did you see anybody today?' Nan asked him as he came in.

Melleron blinked, startled. 'Not a single person,' he said – which was mostly true, since Rose and Grit weren't really *persons*. 'Why?'

'Earlier today,' the old woman said, 'I thought I saw those louts from the village, Jackar and the other two, out on the road. Looking for you, I suppose. Maybe you should stay close to home awhile . . .'

Melleron stiffened. Staying close to home would mean not seeing Rose and Grit, who might think he didn't *want* to see them. And he wasn't going to risk that.

'I don't care about those three,' he said angrily. 'I'm not letting them ruin the summer. I want to go into the forest the same as always.'

Nan smiled. 'Good for you. Anyway, they're probably afraid of the forest, like most folk in the village. The main thing is to stay out of their way.'

I'll be glad to, Melleron thought fiercely.

But over the following few days there was no further sign of the three youths, and no hint of any other trouble. And every day, after the morning chores, Melleron hurried into the forest to find Rose and Grit.

Sometimes Nan went into the forest as well, to gather moon-mushrooms or cut firewood, and then Rose and Grit would stay hidden. But Nan never stayed long, and afterwards Melleron and his new friends would wander the paths, talking merrily, sealing their friendship as the days went on.

But that happiness was interrupted, one day, when Melleron was taking a hoe to more tangleweed in the garden. He heard the scrape of a boot, turned – and froze.

Jackar and his two friends were standing a few feet away, grinning evilly.

CHAPTER 9

Fear in the forest

'Where you been, Ragsy?' Jackar grinned. 'Hidin'?'

'That's what he's gonna get,' Pulce said, snickering. 'A hidin'.'

'An' then some,' Waddel snarled.

Melleron glanced around, but the cottage was silent, as if Nan was having one of her naps. And he knew that the bigger youths could catch him before he got to the door. So as they stepped threateningly forward he braced himself, gripping the hoe tightly, though he knew it wouldn't help much against the three of them.

In that moment the cottage door flew open. Nan stepped out – somehow not looking shaky at all – with a hunting crossbow in her hands, cocked and ready.

'Stop right there,' she said firmly to the youths. 'Get away from this house.'

The youths came to an abrupt halt. Waddel looked wary, Pulce looked nervous, Jackar scowled angrily.

'There's three of us, old hag,' he snarled. 'An' you only got one arrow.'

'That's so,' Nan snapped. 'But you don't know which one of you I'll shoot.'

That made the three take a step back, while Nan stood unmoving, her eyes fierce, her hands steady on the bow. And in the end none of the youths was ready to risk being her target. Muttering oaths and threats, they turned and stamped away.

'If I see you here again,' Nan called after them, 'there'll be shooting first and talking afterwards!'

The youths said nothing, marching sullenly off towards the village, vanishing from sight around a curve in the road.

'Thanks, Nan,' Melleron breathed.

'The *nerve* of them, coming here like that,' she said, lowering the crossbow. Then she frowned thoughtfully. 'You know, Melleron, if they'd do that, they might have the nerve to go after you in the *forest* . . .'

'Oh, I don't think so,' Melleron said quickly. 'And even if they did, I could keep out of their way. I'll be fine, Nan, really.'

The old woman smiled. 'I suppose. You're a good forester. But be careful. Keep your eyes and ears open, all the time.'

'I will, Nan,' Melleron promised. And he hurried to put his hoe away, wanting to go into the forest at once to tell Rose and Grit to be watchful as well, just in case the three bullies did find the courage to go looking for him there.

But when he got into the forest's depths, he couldn't find them.

Usually, those days, Rose and Grit were waiting for him in one of their favourite places. But not that day. And because he was thinking about the youths following him, he didn't want to call out. He just drifted quietly along the paths, searching.

As time passed, and his friends hadn't appeared, he grew more and more unnerved. There was a weird feeling, an *atmosphere,* in that part of the forest. Everything was eerily quiet – no birds singing, no small creatures rustling in the brush. Even the trees seemed to be holding their breath.

Quietly, watchfully, he went on, but Rose and Grit still didn't appear. So by the time he came to the clearing at the heart of the forest, where the ancient iron-oak stood leaning so steeply, he was cold with anxiety. And the clearing was even quieter and more eerie than elsewhere in the forest.

Then he jumped – at the sound of a loud *crunch* from the forest depths nearby, a dry branch snapping. Followed by more crunches and crackles, as if something very big and heavy was pushing through the brush. Towards the clearing.

Melleron didn't think he could get across the clearing and into the forest without being seen, for the sounds were very close. So, instead, he climbed swiftly up the tree itself, helped by the knobbly bark and stumps of dead branches.

Even under his slight weight the tree quivered, as if about to start its final fall. He paused half-way up, not daring to go higher, flattening himself against the trunk. Just as whatever had been crashing in the brush burst out into the clearing.

Melleron nearly shrieked, nearly lost his grip and fell. But utter horror closed his throat and held him motionless.

It was a terrifying monstrosity, enormously tall and bulky, covered in shaggy dark hair, with demonic yellow eyes, curved horns, glittering fangs and claws . . .

Melleron had never seen anything like it before, not even in a nightmare. But he knew its name.

Horrimal.

CHAPTER 10

Into hiding

The monster stamped across the clearing, yellow eyes glittering. Being so huge and terrible, it – *he* – clearly felt no need to move quietly. And he didn't even glance at the tree where Melleron clung, holding his breath and wishing he was invisible.

A moment later, the monster reached the far side of the clearing and crashed back into the greenery. And as the sounds faded in the distance, Melleron could at last take a shuddering breath while nearby birds risked a few nervous chirps.

Clambering shakily down from the iron-oak, Melleron raced away, filled with fear and anxiety. By rights he should tell Nan, or someone, about the monster. Above all, though, he had to find Rose and Grit, and tell *them*.

But at the same time, part of him didn't want to, because Rose and Grit might then flee the forest. And he would lose his new – his *only* – friends.

That dismal thought on top of his shakiness and fright made him blink furiously to hold back tears. Just as Rose whirled out of the forest on to a branch in front of him, while Grit sprang from the brush.

'Melleron!' Rose cried urgently. 'You must get *away! Horrimal* is here!'

'I know,' Melleron broke in. 'I saw him, by the old iron-oak.'

'*Saw* him?' Rose almost shrieked. 'Did he see you?'

'No, I hid,' Melleron said briefly. 'What's he *doing* here?'

'I can only think he must have found out that *we're* here,' Rose said.

Melleron shivered. 'How could he?'

'I don't *know,*' Rose said. 'Maybe through that sorcerer.' She sighed. 'But it means we have to *leave,* now!'

'Rrrr,' Grit growled unhappily.

'Oh, Rose, no . . . !' Melleron cried. Then a thought struck him. 'Why couldn't you just hide, really well, and let me *tell* people? Let *them* get rid of Horrimal!'

Rose shook her head. 'We wouldn't want to be here when the forest was full of people on a *monster* hunt. Anyway, they'd most likely only drive him away – and if he knows we're here, he'd just sneak *back*, later. It's better if we leave.'

'But where could you go?' Melleron asked desperately. 'It's all open farmland and pasture beyond here! You'll never find as good a place to hide as this forest!'

'I don't know . . .' Rose said doubtfully.

'And he's so noisy, he's easy to hide from,' Melleron argued. 'So if you stayed hidden he might *think* you've left, and go looking somewhere else!'

'That's possible . . . ' Rose murmured.

'Rrrr!' Grit said eagerly.

'All right,' Rose decided. 'Grit doesn't want to go, and neither do I. We'll stay and hide awhile, and hope that *he* leaves. So don't tell anyone yet, Melleron.'

Melleron sighed. 'Everything was so lovely these past days,' he said mournfully.

'It will be again,' Rose told him. 'But right now you must hurry home – and stay out of the forest while Horrimal's here.'

'I'll be worried sick every minute,' Melleron said.

'Don't be,' Rose said. 'We won't let him find us. We'll see you again soon.'

With that she and Grit plunged back into the bushes, while Melleron set off home. And because he was full of miseries and worries as he went along, he wasn't paying enough attention to what was happening around him.

So he didn't notice the forest around him becoming quiet, with the eerie stillness of before, as if all its creatures were crouched in silent dread.

Before long he moved around a curve in the path, leading into a gully that held a clear little pond. And he was jolted back to full awareness by a deep, rumbling sound, somewhere between a cough and a grunt.

Beside the pond, the giant shaggy form of Horrimal was stooping to get a drink.

Terror exploded through Melleron like a burst of flame. Whirling, desperately trying to run, he stumbled over a tree-root and fell. And before he could scramble to his feet, Horrimal charged heavily forward, yellow eyes blazing, and grasped his arm with a huge clawed hand.

CHAPTER 11

Fearful meeting

'Why are you creeping around, boy?' he rumbled in a deep cavernous voice.

Melleron was speechless with terror in that mighty grip.

'Speak up!' Horrimal growled. 'Why are you here?'

Still Melleron couldn't move or make a sound.

The monster shook him roughly. 'Listen, runt! When I ask, you answer! Tell me what you are *doing* here!'

'N . . .nothing,' Melleron quavered. 'Walking.'

'Are there more people with you?' Horrimal demanded.

Melleron saw a chance to protect himself. 'There might be,' he said carefully.

Horrimal scowled around at the silent greenery. 'I have seen no one . . .' He raised his massive head, listening. 'Where are they, then?'

'Around somewhere,' Melleron said. 'Nearby.'

Horrimal was silent for a moment, still listening, sniffing the air. 'You lie,' he growled angrily. 'There is no one near.' His immense fangs glinted. 'And you will have no chance to tell people about me, to *bring* them here!'

He strode away from the pool, dragging Melleron roughly along through the brush. But before they reached the path, Horrimal was halted – by a sound like a whimper.

The three bullies from the village were standing farther along the path, staring.

It had been Pulce who whimpered, but all three were rigid with terror. They didn't seem to see Melleron, sprawled among the bushes in the monster's grip. Their wild stares were fixed on Horrimal.

Then they screamed, as Horrimal dropped Melleron and lunged towards them with a roar. And in a panicky scrambling mindless dash the three youths fled, howling, off the path and into the brush.

Pulce tripped and fell on his face in a tangle of netfern. Waddel ran straight into a low thick branch that knocked him flat. Jackar plunged blindly into a wirethorn bush that ripped at his clothing. But even so, they all managed to find their feet and free themselves in time to gallop frantically away before the lumbering Horrimal could reach them.

And during that confusion, Melleron was also racing away into the forest depths.

Despite his own terror, his forester skills avoided all tangles and barriers as he sped through the dimness. Behind him he could hear furious growling from Horrimal – but soon he

slowed, gasping with relief, as he heard the monster crashing away in a totally different direction.

Avoiding all paths, he carefully took a widely roundabout route towards home. With no further sign, all along the way, of Horrimal or the three youths or indeed of Rose and Grit. So before long his fear faded enough that he could even manage a small smile at the memory of the terrified flight of the bullies.

That'll teach them to follow me into the forest, he thought.

But his smile vanished when he realized that the youths would now tell the village about Horrimal. Before long, people would be coming to the forest, armed and determined, to hunt down the monster.

And Rose and Grit wouldn't know that they'd now have to stay hidden from an army of monster-hunters, as well as from Horrimal.

So they had to be told.

He halted, shivering, feeling too frightened to go back right then to find them, with the afternoon shadows growing longer as the sun drifted down towards setting. No matter, he thought. The villagers won't come into the forest after a monster at *night*. There's time. Maybe first thing in the morning . . .

Meanwhile, feeling wrung out and weary after all the terrors of the day, he went along more and more slowly on his long roundabout route, while the sunset reddened the sky and shadows deepened among the trees.

Until he came to another frozen, terrified halt

– when with a rustle of leaves one of the shadows *moved*. Looming out from a clump of trees, towards him.

CHAPTER 12

Deadly trap

'Don't be afraid, Melleron,' said a familiar voice. 'It's me.'

'Nan!' Melleron cried, feeling so weak with relief that he had to lean against a tree-trunk. 'What are you doing here?'

'Looking for you, dear,' the old woman said. 'I was worried.'

Melleron's heart sank. There could be only one reason why Nan would have been worried about him. And that was made even more clear when Melleron saw the grim, troubled look on Nan's face, and the crossbow in her hands.

'Some of the village men rode out to the cottage,' Nan went on, as they headed home. 'Seems those louts who were after you *did* come into the forest. And they went screaming back to the village saying they ran into a huge terrible *monster.*'

'Really?' Melleron said, trying to sound surprised. 'A monster?'

'So they say,' Nan nodded. 'The men also told me there've been attacks on farms in the last day or so. Just like some that have been happening lately west of here. They wanted us to leave the cottage, saying it isn't safe.'

'What did you say?' Melleron asked, alarmed.

Nan snorted. 'I told them no monster's going to scare me out of my home. Then when they left, I came to look for you. But I guess you haven't seen any monsters, or you wouldn't be just ambling along.' She smiled. 'Jackar and those other no-goods were babbling that it's as big as a house with teeth as long as your arm. I reckon they were too scared to see it clearly.'

'Most likely,' Melleron murmured, relieved to know that the youths hadn't seen him, in

Horrimal's grip.

'Anyway,' Nan went on, 'there'll be a troop of villagers with weapons coming into the forest to hunt the creature down.'

'When?' Melleron asked anxiously.

'When they're ready, I expect,' Nan said. 'Some will take a while to work up the nerve, and all of them will waste time muddling and dawdling and arguing, like men do. It'd be a

miracle if they get going in less than a day.' She chuckled. 'Still, it shouldn't be too long before you can go back into the forest.'

But I have to go back tomorrow *morning*, Melleron thought with a shudder.

Arriving home at last, Nan put together a quick supper that Melleron was almost too tired to eat. But in bed later, despite his tiredness, he lay fretfully awake for some time. Despite his concern for Rose and Grit, knowing that he had to warn them that a force of armed humans would soon be in the forest, he didn't feel at all sure that he would be able to do it.

Did he really have the courage to go back into those shadowy depths, knowing that Horrimal was there somewhere?

It occurred to him that Nan wouldn't *allow* him to go into the forest, if she knew he meant to go, and that would be an excuse . . . But at once he felt a surge of guilt. No, he told himself angrily, you can't let that stop you. Or anything else. You have to warn Rose and Grit, it's life and death for them, you *have* to.

I'll slip away when Nan's having a nap, he

thought. And I'll just have to stay out of Horrimal's way. I know the forest better than he does, and he's so careless and noisy I'll hear him before he sees me. It'll be all right. It'll be fine . . .

And so it seemed, the next day, with the sun shining brightly. Nan did decide as usual to have a doze in the late morning – and she didn't actually tell Melleron to stay at home. Clearly she didn't imagine that Melleron would even *think* of going wandering, with a monster on the loose.

So before long Melleron was moving away from the cottage, shivering with dread. For the first time ever he felt afraid, going into his beloved Peaceful Forest, since for once it held a very real danger. But his eyes were fierce with determination, his teeth were clenched so hard that his jaw hurt, and he was not going to let fear stop him from helping his friends.

He decided first to head for the silverberry bushes that Rose visited so often, for even while she was hiding from Horrimal she would still have to eat. It took him some while to reach the grove, for he avoided the paths and all open areas, creeping along one careful tremulous step at a time, trying to make no sound, twitching and sweating with tension.

At least the forest seemed normal, he thought, with none of that eerie stillness of the day before. And he couldn't hear any sounds of something crashing through the brush. Horrimal must be in another part of the forest, he told himself. Maybe asleep in the sun somewhere . . .

The silverberry grove also seemed peaceful, with plenty of berries gleaming on the bushes. But no pink wings were flashing among the leaves, so Melleron crept into the deep shadows beneath the thickest of the bushes, a hideaway where he could safely sit and wait awhile.

By then the peace of the grove, the sounds of the birds and insects, the *normality* of it all, had calmed him a little, easing his tension. So when he heard a rustle nearby, in the shadows, he didn't jump or cower away.

Instead he leaned forward eagerly, peering. 'Rose?' he said softly. 'Grit?'

And then he screamed with stark and desperate terror – as a giant shaggy hand reached through the leaves and clutched him, terrible claws clamping painfully tight to hold him still.

CHAPTER 13

A monstrous threat

'Fool of a boy!' Horrimal rumbled, fangs glinting. 'You dare to come back, after getting away from me yesterday! And now it seems you know the *names* of those two! Are you friends with them? Do you know why they are here?'

Melleron said nothing, moaning with terror and the pain of that fierce grip.

'Well, I will make you tell me later,' Horrimal grinned. 'But what a surprise it was when I spotted the little pink one, yesterday at sunset, flying away from this place! And when I went after her, I found stones on a path that had been chewed by the other one . . . So today I have been here since before first light. If they come, I will be waiting!' His yellow eyes blazed. 'I never expected to find *them* in this forest – or to have my revenge on them so soon!'

Numb and trembling, Melleron nearly wept with despair at the cruel mischance that had let Horrimal spot Rose and Grit. And clearly the monster had been lurking for so long that morning, silent and still, that the birds and small animals of the grove had grown used to him, and had gone back to their normal activity. That was why there had been none of the eerie silence that had alarmed him the day before.

And there *still* isn't, he realized. Rose and Grit could be coming here right now, thinking it's safe . . .

With that dire thought, a wild impulse grasped him.

'Rose!' he screamed at the top of his voice. 'Stay *away*! He's *here* . . . !'

Horrimal's other hand clamped brutally over his mouth. Glaring, the monster peered up through the leaves, before turning back to

Melleron.

'Did you see her?' he rumbled furiously. 'Or are you just hoping she will hear?'

Melleron clutched at a scrap of courage. 'I'm sure she heard me,' he said. 'Sound carries a long way in the forest.'

Horrimal snorted. 'No matter. I will catch them another day.'

He surged to his feet, keeping hold of Melleron – and all around the grove, the forest fell once more into its fearful silence.

'Let me *go!*' Melleron cried, struggling hopelessly.

'Oh, no,' the monster snarled. 'I will keep you. I may use you as *bait*, to trap your little friends. And someone else will also have a use for you . . .'

Effortlessly he lifted Melleron, tucked him under one great arm and stamped away.

Melleron still tried to struggle, but he was gripped so powerfully that he could barely move. He could also barely breathe, with his face pressed into the rank hair of the monster's chest. And something hard was hurting his cheek . . . Pulling his head back, he saw a green stone hanging like a pendant from Horrimal's neck.

'Be still,' Horrimal growled as he crashed on through the forest. 'You cannot get away.' He chortled cruelly. 'You will *never* get away!'

New terror flooded through Melleron, and his struggles weakened, not helped by trying to breathe through the stink of the monster's matted hair. So they went on for a time, until Melleron was suddenly dropped – on to a pile of leaves, in a hollow made by a tangle of three fallen trees, deep in a thicket of honeybriars. The monster's lair.

At once Melleron tried to scramble away. But Horrimal pinned him down with a huge foot, then pulled a long vine away from where it was growing on one of the fallen trees. Dazedly, through his terror, Melleron recognized it. A cable-vine, as flexible as a rope but as strong as woven cable – the toughest plant in the forest.

Wrapping the vine twice around Melleron's

upper body, pinning his arms to his sides, Horrimal knotted it tightly, tying the trailing end to one of the fallen trees.

Then he tore leaves from a bush, jammed them into Melleron's mouth, and used a stringy length of flag-grass to tie them in place as a gag.

'That will keep you quiet,' he rumbled. 'Now I can see if this works . . .'

He lifted up his pendant, looking like a tiny green pebble in his giant hand. 'You know what this is, boy?' he said proudly. '*Magic*. Given to me by my friend Saelez, the sorcerer, who has helped me, covering my tracks while I make war on your people.' He grinned evilly. 'Do you know that Saelez was driven out by your kind because he stole *children* to practise spells on? He will be pleased with *you!'*

Melleron felt as if his body had been wrapped in ice. Rigid with terror, unable to move or speak, he stared wildly as Horrimal raised the stone.

'*Saelez!'* he growled.

Nothing happened. The monster peered around, then scowled down at the stone. 'Saelez!' he roared impatiently.

Then his yellow eyes widened, as a small cloud of pale mist appeared in mid-air, hovering – with the face of a man in the midst of it. Half-hidden by a purple hood, the face was narrow and pasty-grey, with deep-set eyes and a thin-lipped mouth.

'What do you want?' the misty image complained. 'I'm busy.'

'So am I,' Horrimal rumbled. 'Listen. Two small creatures from my homeland are hiding in this forest – the very ones who betrayed me and caused me so much trouble. I want some magic to help me find them.'

The face in the mist twisted with annoyance. 'I can't just *send* you that sort of magic. I would have to come myself – and I have no wish to. I'll help you with ravaging the land and attacking people, but I'm *not* sitting around in a damp forest helping you hunt vermin.'

'But it would be much easier with magic, Saelez,' Horrimal said. 'And I have a gift for you, if you come.'

He pointed down at Melleron. The image in the cloud peered, then showed grey teeth in a ghastly smile. 'A child! How did you get him?'

'He fell into my hands,' Horrimal chortled. 'You can collect him when you come to help me.'

'In that case, I'll come at once!' Saelez said eagerly, staring at Melleron, licking his thin lips. 'I might try an enslaving spell on him. I'd *enjoy* having a slave . . .'

With that the small cloud vanished, and Horrimal grinned down at Melleron. 'You will be wishing you stayed safe at home, boy. And your little friends will wish the same, when I have them in my hands.'

And with a rumble of cruel laughter he strode away.

CHAPTER 14

Desperate flight

Alone, Melleron felt utterly beyond all hope. Nan had said that the villagers would be slow to get moving, so they'd probably arrive too late. Nothing could help Rose and Grit, nothing could save him from being enslaved.

Squeezing his eyes shut against the tears that threatened to fill them, he began another frantic, despairing struggle. He had no chance of breaking the vine – a strong man with a sharp knife would have had a hard time cutting it. He had little chance of loosening the knots tied by Horrimal's mighty hands. Yet still he fought, groaning behind the gag, thrashing around on the ground, while the grip of the cable-vine seemed to grow even tighter.

Until a clear voice said, 'Melleron, don't. Be still.'

And he stopped thrashing and stared with amazement as Rose and Grit slipped quietly into the dark hollow where he lay.

Carefully Rose slid a small claw under the length of grass that held his gag, and jerked downwards. The grass snapped and fell away, and with relief Melleron spat out the mouthful of leaves.

'Rose!' he gasped. 'Horrimal knows you and Grit are here – and he's bringing a *sorcerer* to help him find you! And the sorcerer's going to make me a *slave* . . . !'

'No, he isn't,' Rose said firmly. 'We won't *let* him.'

'Rrrr,' Grit growled in agreement.

Melleron blinked, amazed by their calmness. 'How did you find me?' he asked.

'We were quite near the silverberry grove,' Rose said, 'when we heard you call out.' Her blue eyes softened. 'That was such a *brave* thing to do, Melleron . . .'

'Rrrr,' Grit agreed again.

'So we hid and watched Horrimal go by, carrying you,' Rose went on. 'Then we followed, tracking him by the *noise* he makes.'

'I'm very glad to see you,' Melleron said fervently. 'But I don't know how you can help me, with this vine . . .' He peered at Rose. 'Could you burn through it?'

'Only if I get furious,' Rose said. 'That's what turns on my flame, remember? But I might burn you, too. So I'll leave it to Grit.'

'But it's *cable*-vine!' Melleron said dismally. 'It's unbreakable!'

Rose smiled. 'Watch.'

Grit smiled as well, showing the sharp glittering diamonds that were his teeth. Then he carefully closed those teeth on a loop of the vine just next to where it was knotted at Melleron's side – and bit down hard.

At first nothing happened, though Grit was twisting his head from side to side, growling, gnawing at the vine with all the strength of his powerful jaws. But just as Melleron was about to say that it was hopeless, the cable-vine crackled slightly and fell away, sheared through.

'I knew he could do it,' Rose said, smiling.

'Rrrr!' Grit said proudly.

But then they fell silent. From deep in the forest they heard a terrifying roar, full of vengeful fury. From Horrimal.

'He sounds angry,' Rose said calmly. 'I expect he's found out about the *people* in the forest.'

'People?' Melleron echoed, brightening. 'That's what I came to tell you about! They're really here? Already?'

'A *huge* lot of them,' Rose said, 'with pikes and crossbows. We saw them a while ago, when they were just coming to the edge of the forest.'

Melleron grinned. 'They've come sooner than Nan thought. *They'll* fix Horrimal.'

'Perhaps not,' Rose said. 'Horrimal isn't likely to make a *stand* against so many. He'll *run*.'

'Rrrr, rrrr,' Grit said.

'That's right, Grit,' Rose said quickly. 'He'll probably come *here* first, to get you, Melleron. So *we* must run, too.'

As they hurried away, Melleron's thoughts were racing even faster. If the monster fled from the forest, the people would go home, believing the job was done. But then Horrimal, now knowing that Rose and Grit were there, could simply return – perhaps with Saelez! – and start hunting them all over again.

'I wish I could think of something,' he panted unhappily as they rushed along. 'Some way to get rid of Horrimal for good.'

'I know,' Rose said, drifting among the branches just above him. 'There *should* be something we can do, but I can't think of anything.' She sighed sadly. 'Grit and I may still have to *leave*, Melleron.'

Melleron drooped unhappily at that, half-stumbling over a clump of honeybriar. There must be some other way, he told himself miserably. Maybe the villagers will catch Horrimal and put him in a cage. Or finish him off . . .

Then his spine turned cold, his hair prickling. Behind them – terrifyingly close – they could hear the thrashing noises of Horrimal barging through the forest. As if he was following, directly on their trail.

'He's just behind us!' Melleron gasped.

'But he doesn't know we're here,' Rose said calmly. 'He's *running*, and he just happens to be heading this way.'

They changed direction, so Horrimal would pass without seeing them. And that new route soon brought them to the edge of the broad clearing, deep in the forest, where the old dying iron-oak leaned ever more steeply. Where nothing else grew except grass and flowers – which might hide Grit but not Melleron or Rose.

'We'll have to go *around,*' Rose whispered. 'We don't want to be caught out there in the open.'

Melleron nodded, gazing at the ancient tree. 'Wouldn't it be good,' he muttered fiercely, 'if Horrimal came this way, and the tree fell on him . . .'

'I can't hear him any more,' Rose murmured as they set off again, circling through the brush around the clearing. 'He must be heading *away* from us now . . .'

But a moment later they discovered that she was wrong.

With a bone-freezing roar, Horrimal lunged out of a thicket, clutching at Grit with a massive hand, as Rose shrieked and Melleron yelled with fright.

CHAPTER 15

Impossible idea

'Fools,' the monster growled. 'The breeze carries your scent – and I can move silently when I wish. Now . . .'

But he didn't finish. With a furious growl of his own, Grit twisted and sank his diamond fangs into the huge hand that gripped him. Bellowing, Horrimal jerked his hand away, stumbling back.

'*Run!*' Rose screamed. 'I'll hold him off!'

She flashed down at Horrimal's frightful face, wings beating and claws flailing, as Melleron and Grit turned and ran.

Their flight took them out into the clearing, towards the iron-oak. But Horrimal came crashing after them. Rose was swirling around him, and he was swiping at her like a man pestered by a fly, but he was hardly being slowed down by her at all.

She *can't* hold him off, Melleron thought in terror. She isn't big or strong enough to trouble him.

By then they had reached the tree – where Grit stopped. Ducking among a tangle of crooked roots, pulled partly out of the ground as the tree sagged, Grit crouched, growling softly. As if lying in wait, planning to ambush the monster.

Despite his terror, Melleron flung himself down among the roots as well. Above him a stray gust of wind tugged at the old tree, making it shudder and groan. But Melleron barely noticed – because in that moment, on the edge of the clearing, he saw one of

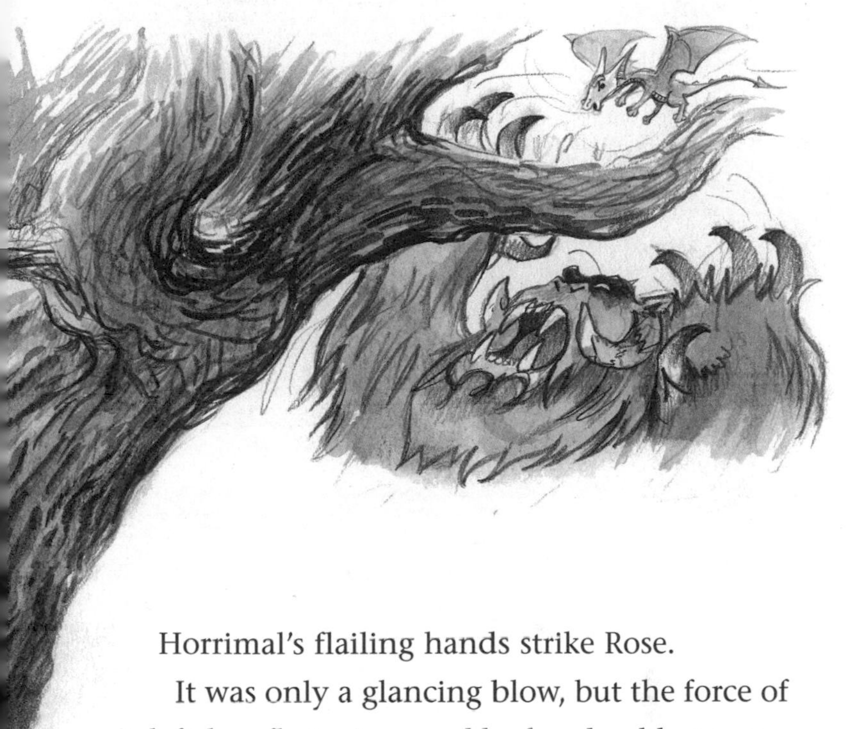

Horrimal's flailing hands strike Rose.

It was only a glancing blow, but the force of it left her fluttering weakly, barely able to stay out of reach as the monster clutched at her.

In desperation Melleron leaped wildly to his feet. 'Come on, *pinky!'* he screamed. '*Fight* him!'

Even half-stunned as she was, Rose heard the hated word. It jolted her out of her daze, so that she swooped away from the terrible reaching hand. And it flung her into a literally blazing fury.

'Not pink, *not pink!'* she shrieked. And a

blistering stream of blue fire gushed from her mouth – into Horrimal's snarling face.

With a roar of pain, Horrimal fell back, slapping at his forehead where the matted hair had caught fire. Then he lunged at Rose again, to be met with more of her fury. Around and around the two of them went, the monster striking and slashing, the little dragon swirling out of reach with her blue flame lancing.

In that frantic moment Grit again seemed

ready to leap out and join the fight. But Melleron went oddly still, a strange light in his eyes.

Another gust of wind had made the old leaning tree creak and lurch again. And that time Melleron noticed it – and had a wild, terrifying idea.

'Grit!' he said quickly. 'Come and *dig!* If we can make Horrimal come this way, maybe we can bring the tree down on him!'

He snatched up a stout stick and began frantically digging under the exposed roots. Grit looked puzzled, but joined in – with astonishing effect.

The soil had been loosened by the upward pull on the tree's roots, and Grit's small but powerful paws were armed with claws like granite. He seemed to sink into the ground, so rapidly did he dig a widening hole. And as he dug, the tree shuddered and creaked even more.

'Can you bite through some of the roots?' Melleron gasped, also digging hard.

'Rrrr!' Grit said, and his diamond teeth clashed. A root gave way, then another, and the

tree groaned and wavered.

'Stop, stop!' Melleron gasped. 'We don't want it to fall yet!'

By then the tree was sagging a great deal more, and its creaking was growing even louder. But not as loud as the roars of Horrimal.

Peering past the tree, Melleron saw that the monster was still striking and clawing at Rose while she dodged and spat more flame. But the battle on the far edge of the clearing was swinging back towards the brush. The wrong way.

Melleron leaped out from among the roots,

into the open. As he did so, the giant tree above him gave a huge lurch, as if finally falling. Heart in mouth, Melleron stared up – but the tree came to rest, still holding its uneasy balance.

Down in the hole they had dug, Grit raised a paw, patted two roots, snapped his bright teeth together, then moved his foreleg sharply downward. Melleron blinked, then understood.

Grit was saying that when he bit through those two roots, the tree would fall.

'Wait!' Melleron said desperately. Then he looked again towards the battle on the clearing's edge. *'Rose!'* he screamed. *'Here!* Come to the *tree!'*

Hearing his cry, Rose hovered for an instant in mid-air, staring with puzzlement in his direction.

Just long enough for Horrimal to strike.

The mighty hand hit her a brutally powerful blow – which flung her, as limp as a discarded cloth, into a bush beyond the clearing.

CHAPTER 16

Final fall

As Horrimal moved menacingly after her, Melleron rushed wildly out into the middle of the clearing, with Grit beside him, growling.

'Leave her *alone*, you big ugly stinking pile of filth!' Melleron yelled.

The monster whirled, roared and bared his fangs. But as Grit crouched, ready to leap into battle, Melleron stopped him.

'No, Grit!' he whispered urgently. 'Let him come! Go back to the *tree* and wait for him! Wait for the right moment – then bring it down!'

Grit blinked, then bounded back towards the

tree, just as Horrimal started towards them. At once Melleron also began to run. But a tuft of long grass seemed to trip him up, and he fell with a cry.

When he got up, he was hobbling painfully, as if he had damaged an ankle.

And with a savage bellowing laugh, Horrimal came thundering across the clearing.

Limping and gasping, Melleron struggled towards the tree while the monster charged towards him. For an instant Grit appeared over the edge of the hole they had dug, ready to help. But Melleron flapped a hand at him.

'No, Grit!' he said through clenched teeth. 'Stay by the roots!'

Grit ducked back, Melleron stumbled on, Horrimal drew closer. The terror-filled moment seemed to stretch out endlessly, as if time had been suspended. And in their total involvement, all three of them failed to hear the sounds that were coming from the forest beyond the clearing.

A great deal of rustling and crackling. As if from many moving feet . . .

In fact, Melleron was so fixed on what he was trying to do that he seemed hardly to be paying attention even to the monster, who was almost upon him.

Must get it *right,* he told himself desperately. Only one chance – must be *exactly* the right place, the right moment . . .

Here, he thought. *Now*.

His hobbling run halted – directly under the sagging, leaning tree. Whirling, he stared at the snarling monster, only two paces and a leap away.

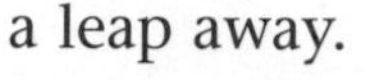

'Now, Grit!' he gasped. *'Now!'*

The words startled Horrimal. He took one pace, then hesitated suspiciously.

In that quivering instant Melleron heard two firm crunches, as Grit's teeth bit through the tree's last two roots.

And with a grinding, wrenching groan like a deep sigh of relief, the old tree fell.

Melleron, no longer hobbling, flung himself sideways with frantic speed, away from the danger. But shock held Horrimal still as if glued to the spot.

And the full weight of the massive old tree fell crushingly, flatteningly, upon him.

Scrambling to his feet, triumphant and delighted, Melleron sprang to the huge hole where the roots had been ripped up. 'Grit, *we did it . . . !*'

But he was talking to an empty space. Grit was no longer there. And as he turned to look for the little dog, Melleron froze with surprise.

On the far edge of the clearing, a troop of armed people – with his Nan among them – stood wide-eyed and open-mouthed, staring at him.

As he saw them, the troop surged forward. But despite her age, Nan got there first.

'Oh, my dear!' she cried, wrapping Melleron in a fierce hug. 'I thought you were dead for sure!'

'Did you see what happened?' Melleron asked anxiously.

'We got here just as the monster caught up with you, under the tree,' Nan said. 'I nearly died myself! Why *ever* did you come into the forest, with that thing around?'

'I . . . I thought I could stay out of its way,' Melleron said vaguely.

'It seems you couldn't,' said a stern voice, and Melleron turned to see the tall figure of Judge Aldin. 'You're lucky to be alive, my boy.'

'What happened to your leg, Melleron?' Nan asked. 'You were limping . . .'

'Er . . . nothing,' Melleron said. 'I was pretending. Like a tree-mouse does.'

The judge blinked. 'Pretending? You *wanted* the monster to chase you?'

Melleron was thinking quickly. Grit had got away through the grass without being seen, and there was still no sign of Rose. So their secret was safe – and had to stay that way.

'Sort of,' he told the judge. 'To bring it under the tree.'

'But how did you know the tree would *fall*?' Nan asked.

Melleron pointed to the stick he had used, with damp earth clinging to one end. 'I did some digging around the roots, with that.'

'Do you mean,' the judge asked, astounded, 'you *made* this happen? Got the tree ready to fall, then *lured* the monster into the right place underneath it?'

'Er . . . yes,' Melleron said. 'Sort of.'

They all went quiet, staring at him. In the silence Melleron saw his three enemies, Jackar, Pulce and Waddel, among the troop. They were gaping at him like the others, with something like awe. And they dropped their eyes, unable to meet his gaze.

'One young boy, doing all that,' the judge breathed. 'Facing the monster alone . . . And the *risk*, the *timing* . . . I wouldn't believe it if I hadn't seen it!'

'Melleron, you're a *hero!*' Nan cried.

As the crowd murmured agreement, a man peered under the tree, then prodded with his boot at the monster's massive, limp leg. 'What'll we do about this?' he asked.

But as he spoke, a hoarse rumbling groan rose from beneath the tree.

'It's *alive!*' someone shouted.

The startled people raised their weapons. Then they were startled again, as a shrill cry echoed across the clearing. A swallow-hawk flashed towards them, swooping down to land on the fallen tree.

But as it settled, it *changed*.

In its place, standing on the tree, was a thin man in a stained purple cloak – his narrow pallid face half-hidden by a hood, his shadowed eyes glittering.

CHAPTER 17

Peace restored

Stunned, the crowd stood like statues as the cloaked man stepped down from the tree, then laid a skinny hand on a branch and spoke a strange word. With that the whole enormous mass of the tree *moved,* rolling heavily to one side.

And from beneath it, from the deep dent that he had made when hammered into the turf, Horrimal sat slowly up.

Blinking dazedly at the armed people, the monster struggled to his feet, swaying as if still half-stunned – while the sorcerer glared at him.

'Be gone,' he told Horrimal sharply. 'You've displayed enough stupidity for one day. There's nothing more to be done here.'

His voice jolted the crowd from its astonished stillness. 'That's Saelez, the sorcerer!' a man shouted. 'The child-stealer!' a woman cried angrily. 'He's *helpin'* the monster!' another man yelled.

With a roar, the crowd lunged forward. But the sorcerer spat another ugly word, sweeping a hand through the air – and a line of hissing green flame leaped high from the grass, so that the people fell back in fright.

'*Go*, you fool!' Saelez snapped furiously at Horrimal. 'While you can!

As the monster lumbered swiftly away, vanishing into the forest, Saelez turned back. Glaring through the veil of eerie fire, he began to lift a bony hand in Melleron's direction. But then he paused. The fire was beginning to shrink, the furious people were gathering themselves . . .

Lowering his hand, Saelez grinned – a chilling, ghastly grin, full of malice and cruelty and a terrible unspoken threat. Then he spread his arms, and was suddenly the swallow-hawk again, arrowing into the air with another shrill cry.

As he vanished, so did the green fire. For a moment the crowd was still – but then someone yelled, 'Come on! That monster won't have got far!' And most of them raced away, leaving Melleron with a few older ones, including Nan and Judge Aldin.

'Whether they catch it or not,' the judge said firmly, 'I don't think that creature will be back this way.'

'Saelez neither,' Nan agreed.

But Melleron, thinking of the threat in the sorcerer's grin, was not so sure.

'And now,' the judge said, smiling, 'on our way home, we can talk about how the village might show its appreciation to our young hero, here.'

But as they set off, Melleron held back. 'I'll catch you up,' he told Nan. 'I have to . . . find something.'

'Don't be long,' she said. 'It's near dinnertime.' Then she went on, while Melleron dashed in the other direction – towards the bush where Rose had fallen.

'Rose? Grit?' he called softly as he plunged

into the brush. 'Where are you?'

'Here!' said a clear voice, and Rose swooped down from a treetop as Grit popped out from a cluster of ferns.

'Rose!' Melleron cried. 'You're not hurt!'

'Just bruised,' she said brightly. 'He hit me *very* hard. But the tree hit him a lot harder!' She flapped her wings joyfully. 'You two were *brilliant* – it all worked so *wonderfully* . . .'

'Until Saelez came,' Melleron muttered.

'But now they're gone,' Rose laughed. 'The forest is peaceful again. So we don't have to leave our friend!' She smiled teasingly. 'And I don't have to leave the *silverberries* . . .'

That made them all laugh. And in the midst of the laughter, Nan stepped quietly from behind a bush, wide-eyed, and said, 'What on earth . . . ?'

'Nan!' Melleron gasped as he and his friends froze.

'I wondered what was keeping you,' Nan said, still staring. 'But I never expected anything like this. What *are* they?'

'Friends,' Rose said brightly. 'We're Melleron's

friends. And we're *very* happy to meet his grandmother.'

'Are you?' Melleron asked, startled. 'You're supposed to be a secret!'

'You haven't told anyone, Melleron,' Rose said. 'I don't think *she* will either.'

'Not if you don't want me to,' Nan said dazedly.

With that, also feeling a little dazed, Melleron introduced Rose and Grit to Nan, explaining about them and why they were there.

'Well, I never,' Nan said, shaking her head. 'A dog made of stone, and a dragon who's such a nice colour, a really pretty . . .'

'Don't say it!' Melleron cried.

Nan blinked. 'What? I was just going to say, she's the colour of the *roses* I used to grow by the cottage.'

Rose laughed. 'I think we're going to get on very well,' she said to Nan.

'Rrr,' Grit said with a bright-toothed grin.

'And so you two were helping Melleron with the tree and all,' Nan said. 'That explains why it all happened so perfectly!'

'I was helping them, really,' Melleron said.

'We were helping each *other,'* Rose said merrily. 'As friends do.'

'Well, now,' Nan said wonderingly. Then she smiled. 'Why don't we all go back to the cottage for something to eat, and get to know each other better?'

'Er . . . Rose eats fruit,' Melleron told her, 'and Grit eats *stone.'*

'Goodness,' Nan said, raising her eyebrows. 'Well, we have lots of fruit, and there's a heap of flints that were dug out of the garden.'

'Perfect!' Rose cried.

'Rrrr!' Grit said, wagging his tail.

So the four of them set off together. While all around them birds chirped and insects buzzed and leaves rustled, as if applauding, throughout the Peaceful Forest.

About the author

When I was young I was always getting lost – but not outside. I got lost in books, especially in the enchanting worlds of fantasy and science fiction. Now I'm no longer young, I write such stories, and still get lost in them.

Also, I've always loved woodlands. So when I dreamed up the idea of a boy and some unusual monsters, their adventure just had to happen in a forest. I was happily lost there, writing the story. I hope you were, too, reading it.